Ninja Blender Recipe Book

Lose Weight And Shred The Pounds Fast With These Delicious And Healthy Ninja Blender Recipes You Can Make Tonight!

of the information is without contract or any type of guarantee assurance.

Cover image courtesy of Ken Hawkins – City Java Smoothies – Flickr -

Table of Contents

Want more books?

Would you love books delivered straight to your inbox every week?

Free?

How about non-fiction books on all kinds of subjects?

We send out e-books to our loyal subscribers every week to download and enjoy!

All you have to do is join! It's so easy!

Just visit the link at the end of this book to sign up and then wait for your books to arrive!

Introduction

I want to thank you for purchasing the book, "Ninja Blender Recipe Book: *Lose Weight And Shred The Pounds Fast with These Delicious and Healthy Ninja Blender Recipes You Can Make Tonight*".

Ninja Blenders are a lifesaver! Not only can you muddle up ingredients as required, you now have the luxury to let your Ninja blender separate pits from the fruits for you. Ninja Blenders are very easy to use, all it takes is a press of a button, and that's it.

I have used Greek yogurt in most of these recipes instead of regular yogurt as the former has twice the protein than regular and usually half the sugar, which makes it perfect when you're on a diet. I have replaced sugar with honey and fresh fruits, but if you prefer you may replace the sweetening agent with other sugar substitutes or even brown sugar.

I hope you enjoy your way to good health with these delicious weight loss Ninja blender recipes. Losing weight never tasted so good!

Thanks again, I hope you enjoy this book!

Lemon Meringue Pie

Ingredients

- 1 cup lemonade

- ½ cup lemon flavored yogurt

- 2 oz cream cheese

- 6-8 ice cubes

- lemon zest and mint leaves for garnish

Preparation

1. Pour lemonade, yogurt, cream cheese, ice cubes in the Ninja blending jar and churn it to a desired consistency.

2. Pour the mixture in tall chilled glasses and garnish with lemon zest and mint leaves.

Diet Smoothie

Ingredients

- 2 beetroots peeled and chopped
- 2 large carrot, peeled and chopped
- 2 cucumbers, peeled
- 2 green apples
- 2 large tomatoes
- 1 sprig fresh mint leaves
- 1 sprig fresh parsley leaves
- 1 tsp lime juice
- ¼ tsp salt
- ½ Tbs white pepper powder
- 1 ½ cup Greek yogurt

Preparation

1. In the Ninja blender combine beetroots, carrots, cucumbers, apples, tomatoes, mint leaves, parsley, limejuice, salt, pepper and Greek yogurt in, until the texture turns into a silky texture.

2. Pour the contents in chilled glasses and serve chilled.

Chilled Blueberry Blast

Ingredients

- 1 1/2 cup white grape juice
- 1 1/2 cup low fat yogurt
- 1 1/2 banana
- 1 1/2 cup fresh blueberries
- 8-10 ice cubes
- mint leaves for garnish

Preparation

1. Add grape juice, yogurt, banana and blueberries into the Ninja blender with ice and process until the mixture is smooth.

2. Serve it in tall chilled glasses and garnish with mint leaves.

Zesty Orange Creamsicle

Ingredients

- 2 cups oranges, peeled and de-seeded
- 4tbs orange concentrate, frozen preferred
- 1/2 tsp vanilla essence vanilla bean extract
- 8-10 ice cubes
- 1cup Greek yogurt, fat free
- 1 ½ Tbs rum, optional

Preparation

1. Add navel oranges, frozen orange concentrate, vanilla bean extract, ice cubes, and Greek yogurt in the Ninja blender until smooth.

2. You could add rum while blending the smoothie or, pour the drink in glasses and choose to flambé the drink for a crusty bittersweet after taste.

3. Pour in tall chilled glasses and serve.

Tropical Passion Smoothie

Ingredients

- 1 cup canned pineapples, discard syrup

- 1 cup Greek yogurt

- 1 kiwi, chopped

- 5-6 Strawberries

- 6-8 ice cubes

Preparation

1. In the Ninja blender, add canned pineapples, Greek yogurt, kiwi, strawberries, and ice cubes until smooth.

2. Pour the drink in chilled glasses and serve chilled.

Banana Delight Smoothie

Ingredients

- 1 cup skimmed milk
- 2 large bananas, chopped
- ½ Tbs vanilla extract or vanilla essence
- ½ Tbs cocoa powder
- 2 Tbs honey
- ½ Tbs powdered Peanut Butter
- ¼ cup hazelnuts, coarsely chopped
- ½ cup ice cubes
- A pinch cinnamon powder, for garnishing

Preparation

1. Blend skimmed milk, bananas, vanilla extract, and cocoa powder, honey, and ice cubes until smooth in the Ninja blender.
2. Pour the smoothie in a tall glass, add chopped hazelnuts, and dust some cinnamon powder over it. Serve chilled.

Fruit Jelly Smoothie

Ingredients

- 1 ½ cup skimmed milk

- 2 large bananas

- 2 Tbs peanut butter

- 2 tsp flax seeds

- 2 ½ blueberry jelly

- 6-8 ice cubes

- 2 Tbs honey, (optional)

Preparation

1. In the Ninja blender, add skimmed milk, bananas, peanut butter, flax seeds, blueberry jelly, until it forms smooth texture.
2. Pour the smoothie in chilled glasses and top with honey and serve chilled.

Tomato-Basil Smoothie

Ingredients

- 6 large tomatoes, chopped
- 1 cup radish, peeled and chopped
- 1 sprig mint leaves
- ¼ tsp sea salt
- ¼ tsp white pepper powder
- 5-6 basil leaves
- 1 juice of lime
- 1 tsp ginger concentrate
- 1 green chili, (optional)
- 8-10 cup ice cubes

Preparation

1. Blend tomatoes, radish, mint leaves, sea salt, white pepper, basil leaves, limejuice, green chili, ginger concentrate and ice cubes until smooth.

2. Pour the drink in tall chilled glasses, garnish with mint leaves, and serve chilled.

Banana and Ginger Smoothie

Ingredients

- 2 large bananas

- 1 ½ Tbs concentrated ginger

- 2 Tbs brown sugar or honey, (optional)

- 6-8 ice cubes

- 1 cup Greek yogurt

Preparation

1. Combine bananas, fresh grated ginger, brown sugar, ice cubes, and Greek yogurt in the Ninja blender until it forms a creamy and silky consistency.

2. Pour the smoothie in tall chilled glasses and serve chilled.

Herbal Tea and Berries Smoothie

Ingredients

- 1 cup water

- 1 herbal tea bag

- 2 ½ tsp honey

- 1 tsp frozen concentrated ginger extract

- 1 ½ cup mixed berries, fresh

- 1 medium sized bananas, chopped

- ½ cup skimmed milk

- 6-8 ice cubes

- mint leaves for garnish

Preparation

1. In a pot, boil water and prepare herbal tea.

2. Remove the tea bag from the pot and add honey to the tea, and stir. Allow it to cool at room temperature.

3. Combine brewed green tea, frozen ginger concentrate, mixed berries, bananas, and skimmed milk with ice cubes until smooth.

4. Pour the mix in glasses, garnish with mint leaves, and serve chilled.

Spiced Pumpkin with Cream Smoothie

Ingredients

- 1 cup fresh pumpkin chunks pumpkin puree

- 2 cup Greek Curd /almond/vanilla milk

- ½ Tbs nutmeg powder

- 3 Tbs almonds, roasted and coarsely chopped

- 3 Tbs dates, cored and chopped

- ¼ Tbs cinnamon powder

- ½ tsp ginger root, peeled and grated

- ¼ Tbs salt

- ¼ cup pumpkin, grated, chopped or diced (optional) for a topping

- 1 cup ice cubes

- mint leaves, for garnish

Preparation

1. Add fresh pumpkin chunks, Greek Curd, nutmeg powder, chopped almonds, walnut, cinnamon spice ginger, ice cubes, and salt in a blender until it turns into an orange, creamy texture.

12

2. Pour the smoothie in tall glasses, and top it with some left over roasted almonds and walnuts.

3. Finally add chopped mint leaves as topping and serve in tall chilled glasses.

Summer Coolers Smoothie

Ingredients

- 2 cups cucumbers, peeled and chopped (preferably chilled)
- ¼ Tbs sea salt
- 1 sprig fresh celery, chopped
- ¼ cup mint leaves
- 1 cup soda
- 1 Tbs lime juice

Preparation

1. In the Ninja blender add cucumbers, sea salt, chopped celery, mint leaves, soda and lime juice until it turns into a green blend.

2. Pour in chilled glasses, garnish with mint leaves, and serve chilled.

Cupid's Smoothie

Ingredients

- ½ cup cranberry juice

- 1 cup strawberries, fresh and chopped

- ½ cup pineapple juice, chilled

- 1 cup kiwi, peeled and chopped

- ½ tsp cinnamon powder

- 2 scoops vanilla ice cream

- 2 Tbs honey

- 2 tsp white chocolate, grated

Preparation

1. For the first layer, blend cranberry juice and strawberries in the Ninja blender and pour the mixture in a tall glass.
2. For the second layer blend pineapple juice, kiwifruit, and cinnamon powder until smooth.
3. Gently add a scoop of vanilla ice-cream over the first layer in the glass.
4. Pour the second layer over the ice-cream and top it with honey and grated white chocolate. Serve immediately.

Dry Fruit Smoothie

Ingredients

- ½ liter Almond milk, chilled

- 3-4 Tbs honey

- 2 Tbs almonds, chopped

- 2 Tbs cashew nuts, chopped

- 1 Tbs unsalted pistachios

- 2 Tbs walnuts, chopped

- 4 dates, (cored, chopped and soaked warm milk for 20 minutes)

- ¼ tsp pepper powder, optional

- ½ tsp nutmeg, powder

- A pinch of saffron

- rose petals for garnish

Preparation

1. Combine almond milk with honey, chopped almonds, cashew nuts pistachios, walnuts, dates, pepper powder, nutmeg powder, and saffron until they blend well in the Ninja blender.

2. Pour the blend in chilled glasses topped with rose petals and serve chilled.

Tropicana Smoothie

Ingredients

- 1 cup canned pineapple

- ½ cup yellow papaya, chopped

- 2 Tbs coconut milk

- 1 cup Greek yogurt

- 2 Tbs white rum

- 2 tsp fresh cream

- 6-8 cup ice cubes

- 1 vanilla bean extract

- 1 tsp sun flower seeds, optional

Preparation

1. Combine canned pineapples, yellow papaya, coconut extract, Greek yogurt, and white rum, fresh cream, and ice cubes, in the Ninja blender until frosty.

2. Pour the beverage in chilled glasses, and top with crushed flax seeds. Serve chilled.

Fruit Punch Infused with Spice Smoothie

Ingredients

- 1 ½ cup Greek yogurt

- 2 cups bananas, chopped

- 1 ½ cup mango, chopped or mango juice/pulp

- 2 cups canned peaches

- 1 Tbs honey

- ¼ Tbs cinnamon spice

- ¼ Tbs nutmeg powder

- 6-8 ice cubes

- mint leaves, for garnish

Preparation

1. Add the Greek yogurt, bananas, mango, peaches, honey, cinnamon spice nutmeg powder, and ice cubes in the Ninja blender, and churn until it all blends well.

2. Pour the chilled mixture into tall glasses and garnish with mint leaves.

3. You might want to top it with some chopped mangoes while serving, for extra taste. Serve chilled.

Fruity Affair Smoothie

Ingredients

- 1 cup mixed berries, frozen
- ¼ cup Kiwi
- 1 Avocado, peeled and cored
- ¼ cup black grapes, frozen
- 1 Large banana, chopped
- 1 cup canned pineapple juice
- ½ cup orange juice, optional
- 1 cup Greek yogurt
- 5-6 ice cubes

Preparation

1. Blend together mixed berries, kiwi, avocado, frozen black grapes, banana, canned pineapple juice, orange juice and Greek yogurt and blend until smooth in the Ninja blender.

2. Add ice cubes in glasses and pour the drink in it. Top with chopped fruit of your choice and serve chilled.

Peach Smoothie

Ingredients

- 1 cup skimmed milk

- 1 cup Greek yogurt

- 1 cup canned peaches

- 1 cup strawberries, fresh

- ¼ Tbs ginger concentrate

- 5-6 ice cubes

- 2 Tbs honey

- 1 cup marshmallows, optional

Preparation

1. In the Ninja blender, add skimmed milk, canned peaches, fresh strawberries, ginger powder, ice cubes, honey, and marshmallows and thoroughly blend until it forms a smooth and even consistency.

2. Pour the drink in chilled glasses and serve chilled.

Salad Smoothie

Ingredients

- 3 medium sized carrots, peeled and chopped
- ½ cup celery stalks
- 1 large tomato
- 1 large cucumber, peeled and chopped
- 1 radish , peeled and chopped
- 1 tsp lime juice
- ¼ tsp black salt, optional
- 1 cup Greek yogurt
- 8-10 ice cubes
- 6-8 mint leaves
- ¼ Tbs white pepper powder

Preparation

1. In the Ninja blender add chopped carrots, celery stalks, tomato, cucumber, lime juice, black salt, Greek yogurt, and ice cube and mint leaves until it forms a smooth texture.

2. Serve in tall chilled glasses and garnish with white pepper powder.

Rose Smoothie

Ingredients

- 1 cup skimmed milk

- 3 Tbs rose syrup concentrate

- 1/12 Tbs honey

- 8-10 ice cubes

- 2 Tbs almonds, fine chopped

- Tender red rose petals for garnishing

- 2-3 scoops Vanilla ice-cream, optional

Preparation

1. In the Ninja blender add skimmed milk, rose syrup, honey, ice cubes, and blend thoroughly.

2. Pour the pink mix in tall chilled glasses and garnish with chopped almonds and rose petals. Add ice-cream to the drink before garnishing if preferred. Serve immediately.

Halloween Smoothie

Ingredients

- 1 cup marshmallows

- 1 ½ cup pumpkin puree, chilled

- 1 banana, peeled and chopped

- 2 Tbs honey, optional

- 1 cup ice cubes

- 2 Tbs brandy, optional

Preparation

1. Add marshmallows, pumpkin puree, banana, honey, ice cubes and brandy in the Ninja blender until a rich creamy textures is made.

2. Pour the drink in tall chilled classes and serve chilled.

Banana n' Soy Smoothie

Ingredients

- 2 large bananas, chopped
- ¼ cup almonds, roasted and chopped
- ¼ cup dry figs, chopped
- 2 Tbs raisins, soaked in warm soy milk for 20 minutes, de-seeded and chopped
- 2 Tbs honey
- 1 ½ cup soymilk, chilled
- ½ tsp vanilla bean extract
- 5-6 ice cubes, optional
- A pinch of freshly ground nutmeg and cinnamon powder

Preparation

1. Combine bananas, almonds, dry figs, raisins, honey, chilled soymilk and ice cubes in a blender until smooth.

2. Pour in chilled glasses, top with freshly ground spices, and serve.

Devil's Eye Smoothie

Ingredients

- 1 large avocado, peeled, cored and chopped

- 2 cucumber, peeled and chopped

- 1 cup banana, chopped

- 1 cup spinach leaves

- 2 Tbs lime juice

- 1 cup yogurt, low fat

- 8-10 ice cubes

Preparation

1. Add avocados, cucumber, banana spinach leaves, lime juice, yogurt and ice cubes in the Ninja blender until it all turns into an envious green liquid.
2. Pour in chilled glasses and serve chilled.

Bottle Gourd Smoothie

Ingredients

- ½ cup bottle gourd
- ½ cup cucumber
- ½ cup yogurt
- ½ cup silken tofu
- 10-12 cup mint leaves
- 6-8 ice cubes
- ¼ Tbs pepper powder
- ¼ tsp salt

Preparation

1. In the Ninja blender, add bottle gourd, cucumber, yogurt, silken tofu, mint leaves, ice cubes, salt, and pepper until it turns into desired consistency.

2. Pour the drink in tall chilled glasses and serve as a perfect diet breakfast.

Adam n' Eve Smoothie

Ingredients

- 2 large green apples, de-seeded and chopped (do not peel)
- 2 tsp honey
- 2 tsp concentrated ginger syrup
- ¼ tsp nutmeg powder
- 1 sprig parsley leaves, chopped
- 1 cup club soda, chilled
- 8-10 ice cubes
- ¼ cup white rum
- mint leaves, for garnishing

Preparation

1. In the Ninja blender, add apples, honey, concentrated ginger, nutmeg powder, parsley leaves, club soda, ice, and white rum until smooth.

2. Pour the drink in tall chilled glasses and garnish with mint leaves. Serve chilled.

Sinful Strawberry Smoothie

Ingredients

- 2 ½ cups Strawberry, fresh
- 1 cup Greek yogurt, low fat
- 1 tsp lime juice
- ½ cup passion fruit
- ¼ cup mint leaves
- 1 sprig basil leaves
- 8-10 ice cubes
- ½ vanilla bean extract

Preparation

1. Blend strawberries, yogurt, lime juice, passion fruit, mint leaves, basil leaves, ice cubes, and vanilla bean extract until it turns to liquid.

2. Pour the mixture in chilled tall glasses and serve right away.

Raspberry n' Rosemary Smoothie

Ingredients

- ½ Tbs concentrated raspberry syrup
- 1 cup fresh raspberries
- 1 fresh sprig rosemary, chopped
- 1 cup Greek yogurt
- 8-10 ice cubes

Preparation

1. In the Ninja blender combine concentrated raspberry syrup, fresh raspberries, rosemary, Greek yogurt, and ice cubes until it turns frosty.

2. Pour the mixture in tall frozen glasses and serve chilled.

Sapodilla Smoothie

Ingredients

- 2 cups sapodilla, peeled and cored and chopped

- 2 cups skimmed milk

- 8-10 ice cubes

- 2 Tbs honey

- 1 ½ Tbs cocoa powder

- flax/sunflower seeds for garnish

Preparation

1. In the Ninja blender, combine skimmed milk, sapodilla, ice cubes, honey, and cocoa powder until smooth.

2. Pour the mixture in tall chilled glasses, and top with flax seeds and serve chilled.

Summer Delight Smoothie

Ingredients

- 4 cups mangoes, boiled, peeled and cored

- 6 Tbs honey

- 1 Tbs concentrate ginger extract

- ½ Tbs salt

- 1 sprig mint leaves, chopped

- 2 ½ cups chilled water

- 10-12 ice cubes

- ½ Tbs saffron

Preparation

1. In the Ninja blender, add raw mangoes, honey, concentrated ginger extract, salt, mint leaves, chilled water, ice cubes, and saffron until it forms a pale green pulpy texture.

2. Pour half the mix in a glass and the rest with some chilled water.

Custard Apple Smoothie

Ingredients

- 2 large custard apples, fresh, peeled, de-seeded
- 2 ripe bananas
- 2 Tbs honey
- 1 tsp vanilla bean extract
- 1 cup skimmed milk
- ¼ tsp cardamom powder
- ¼ nutmeg powder
- ¼ cup almonds, coarsely chopped
- 1 cup ice cubes

Preparation

1. In the Ninja blender, add custard apples, bananas, honey, vanilla bean extract, skimmed milk, cardamom powder, nutmeg powder, almonds, and ice cubes and churn until smooth.

2. Pour the drink in tall chilled glasses, top with chopped almonds. Serve chilled.

Cilantro Smoothie

Ingredients

- 2 cup Greek yogurt

- 2 Sprigs fresh cilantro

- 1 tsp lime juice

- 2 tsp sesame seeds

- 6-8 mint leaves

- 8-10 ice cubes

Preparation

1. Blend Greek yogurt, fresh cilantro, lime juice, sesame seeds, mint leaves, and ice cubes in the Ninja blender until it turns into a pale green liquid.

2. Pour in chilled tall glasses, garnish with mint leaves, and serve chilled.

Cranberry Smoothie

Ingredients

- 2 ½ cup fresh cranberries

- 2 cup canned pineapples, chopped, discard the syrup

- 1 cup cranberry juice, chilled

- 2 Tbs coconut cream

- 1 cup Greek yogurt

- 8-10 ice cubes

- 2-4 Tbs brown sugar, caramelized

Preparation

1. In the Ninja blender add fresh cranberries, canned pineapples, cranberry juice, coconut cream, Greek yogurt, ice cubes and caramelized brown sugar and blend well.

2. Pour the drink in tall chilled glasses, garnish with some coconut cream, and serve right away.

Grapefruit Smoothie

Ingredients

- 1 cup grapefruit

- 1 green apple

- 1 banana, optional

- 8-10 fresh strawberries

- 1 cup Greek Yogurt

- 1 Tbs fresh ginger, peeled and chopped

- 6-8 ice cubes

Preparation

1. Add grapefruit, green apple, banana, strawberries and Greek yogurt, fresh ginger and ice cubes and churn them all together in the Ninja blender until smooth.

2. Pour the mix in chilled tall glasses and serve right away.

Multivitamin Smoothie

Ingredients

- 2 oranges
- 2 cups spinach
- 1 large cucumber
- 1 cup kale
- 1 Tbs lemon juice
- 2-3 celery stalks
- 8-10 ice cubes

Preparation

1. In the Ninja blender add oranges, spinach, cucumber, kale, lemon juice, celery stalks, ice cubes, and blend them together.

2. Pour the mix in tall chilled glasses and serve.

Fat Burning Smoothie

Ingredients

- 1 cup green tea

- 2 cups cauliflower florets

- 2 cups broccoli florets

- 4 pineapple spears

- ice cubes, optional

Preparation

1. Add green tea, cauliflower, broccoli, and pineapple in the Ninja blender and churn well.

2. Pour the mix into tall chilled glasses and serve with some ice cubes.

Berry Melon Smoothie

Ingredients

- ½ large cantaloupe melon
- 1 ½ cup blueberries
- 1 Tbs flax seeds
- 1 cup skimmed milk
- 8-10 ice cubes

Preparation

1. In the Ninja blender, blend melon, blueberries, flax seeds, and skimmed milk with ice cubes until done well.

2. Pour the drink in tall chilled glasses and serve right away.

Berry Blast Smoothie

Ingredients

- ½ strawberries
- ½ raspberries
- ½ blue berries
- ½ cup rainbow chard
- 1 cup pomegranate
- 1 ¼ cup coconut milk
- 6-8 ice cubes
- mint leaves for garnish

Preparation

1. In the Ninja blender, add strawberries, raspberries, blue berries, rainbow chard, and pomegranate, coconut milk, and ice cubes until it turns deep maroon liquid.

2. Pour the smoothie into tall chilled glasses, garnish with mint leaves, and serve.

Orange and Carrot Smoothie

Ingredients

- 1 cup orange juice, fresh preferably

- 1 cup carrots, peeled and chopped

- 1 Tbs honey

- 1 tsp ginger concentrate, optional

- ½ coconut milk

- 6-8 ice cubes

Preparation

1. In the Ninja blender add orange juice, carrots, honey, ginger concentrate, coconut milk, and ice cubes and blend well.

2. Pour the drink in tall chilled glasses and serve.

Pre-workout Peach Smoothie

Ingredients

- 3 large peaches, remove pit
- 6-8 almonds
- 6-8 walnuts, chopped
- 1 cup almond milk
- ½ cup Greek yogurt
- 2 Tbs honey
- 1 Tbs flax seeds, optional
- 8-10 ice cubes

Preparation

1. In the Ninja blender, add peaches, almonds, walnuts, almond milk, Greek yogurt, flax seeds, and ice cubes until smooth.

2. Pour the smoothie into tall chilled glasses and serve.

Post-workout Berrylecious Smoothie

Ingredients

- 1 ¼ fresh berries

- 1 large banana

- 1 cup soy milk

- 1 Tbs sunflower seeds

- 5-6 ice cubes

Preparation

1. Blend fresh berries, banana, soy-milk, sunflower seeds, and ice cubes in the Ninja blender until smooth.

2. Pour the drink in tall chilled glasses and serve.

Watermelon Smoothie

Ingredients

- 2 cups watermelon, de-seeded and chopped
- 2 cups raspberries
- 2 cups strawberries
- 1 large beetroot
- ¼ Tbs salt
- ¼ white pepper powder
- 1 Tbs honey

Preparation

1. In the Ninja blender add watermelon, raspberries, strawberries, beetroot, salt, pepper powder, honey, ice cubes, and blend well.
2. Pour the drink into tall chilled glasses and serve.

Protein Extravaganza Smoothie

Ingredients

- 1 cup kiwi, peeled and chopped

- 1 cup fresh pineapples, chopped

- 8 almonds

- 4 dates, cored

- 1 ¼ Greek yogurt

- ¼ cup coconut milk

- 1 Tbs protein shake powder

- 8-10 ice cubes

Preparation

1. In the Ninja blender, add kiwi, pineapples, almonds, dates, Greek yogurt, coconut milk, protein shake powder, ice cubes, and blend well.

2. Pour the drink into tall chilled glasses and serve right away.

Papaya Smoothie

Ingredients

- ½ cup papaya, chopped

- 1 large banana

- 5-6 strawberries

- 1 cup almond milk

- 5-6 ice cubes

- mint leaves for garnish

Preparation

1. Blend papaya, banana, strawberries, almond milk, ice cubes in the Ninja blender until smooth.

2. Pour the drink into tall chilled glasses, garnish with mint leaves, and serve right away.

Romaine leaves Smoothie

Ingredients

- 10-15 large leaves Romaine lettuce

- 2 large green apples

- ½ cup musk melon, chopped

- 8-10 ice cubes

Preparation

1. In the Ninja blender add Romaine lettuce leaves, green apples, musk melon, ice cubes, and blend well.

2. Pour the mix into tall chilled glasses and serve.

Mocha Smoothie

Ingredients

- 1 cup Greek yogurt

- 1 shot espresso

- 2 Tbs hazelnuts, chopped

- 1 ½ Tbs cocoa powder

- 5-6 ice cubes

Preparation

1. In the Ninja blender, add Greek yogurt, espresso, hazelnuts, cocoa powder, and ice cubes until they blend well.

2. Pour the mix into tall chilled glasses and serve.

Blueberries Smoothie

Ingredients

- 1 cup blueberries, frozen

- 1 large banana

- ½ Tbs apple juice concentrate

- 1/3 cup soy protein

- 1 tsp flax seeds

- 5-6 ice cubes

- ½ cup Greek yogurt

Preparation

1. Place blueberries, banana, apple juice concentrate, soy protein, flax seeds, ice cubes, Greek yogurt in the Ninja blender and churn well.

2. Pour the drink into tall chilled glasses and serve chilled.

Strawberry-Banana Smoothie

Ingredients

- 1cup Greek yogurt

- 1 cup strawberries, chopped

- 1 banana

- 2 Tbs honey

- 5-6 ice cubes

- mint leaves for garnish

Preparation

1. In the Ninja blender add Greek yogurt, strawberries, banana, honey, ice cubes, and blend well.

2. Pour the drink into tall chilled glasses and garnish with mint leaves, serve chilled.

Honeydew and Kiwi Smoothie

Ingredients

- 2 cups honeydew, chopped

- 2 kiwi fruit, peeled and chopped

- 1 large Granny Smith apple

- 1 Tbs lemon juice

- 2 Tbs honey

- 5-6 ice cubes

- mint leaves for garnish

Preparation

1. In the Ninja blender, place honeydew, kiwi fruit, apples, lemon juice, honey, ice cubes, and churn well.

2. Pour the drink into tall chilled glasses and serve chilled.

Blueberry and Vanilla Yogurt Smoothie

Ingredients

- 3 ounces low fat vanilla yogurt

- 1 ½ cup fresh blueberries

- 1 cup skimmed milk

- 1 Tbs flax seeds

- 8-10 ice cubes

Preparation

1. In the Ninja blender, add vanilla yogurt, blueberries, skimmed milk, flax seeds, ice cubes and churn well.

2. Pour the drink into tall chilled glasses and serve chilled.

Mango Twist Smoothie

Ingredients

- 1 cup ripe mango, chopped

- 1 cup avocado, peeled, cored and chopped

- 1 Tbs lemon juice

- 2 Tbs honey

- 1 cup Greek yogurt

- 8-10 ice cubes

Preparation

1. In the Ninja blender, add ripe mangoes, avocado, lemon juice, honey, Greek yogurt, ice cubes and blend until smooth.

2. Pour the smoothie into chilled glasses and serve chilled.

Raspberry and Chocolate Smoothie

Ingredients

- 1 ½ cups fresh raspberries

- 1/4 cup chocolate chips

- ½ cup soy milk

- 5-6 ice cubes

Preparation

1. In the Ninja blender, churn together, fresh raspberries, chocolate chips, soymilk, ice cubes until smooth.

2. Pour the smoothie into tall chilled glasses and serve right away.

Soymilk and Peach Smoothie

Ingredients

- 2 cups frozen unsweetened peaches

- 2 cups soy milk

- 2 Tbs honey

- 1 Tbs flax seeds

- 5-6 ice cubes

Preparation

1. Add peaches, soymilk, honey, flax seeds, ice cubes in the Ninja blender and churn well.

2. Pour the smoothie into tall chilled glasses and serve.

Orange n' Lemon Citrus Smoothie

Ingredients

- 6 ounces lemon yogurt

- 1 cup skimmed milk

- 1 cup oranges, fresh, peeled and de-seeded'

- ¼ cup mint leaves

- 5-6 ice cubes

Preparation

1. In the Ninja blender, add lemon yogurt, skimmed milk, oranges, mint leaves, ice cubes, and blend well.

2. Pour the drink into tall chilled glasses, garnish with mint leaves, and serve.

Apple Smoothie

Ingredients

- 1 cup skimmed milk

- 4 ounces vanilla yogurt

- ¼ Tbs cinnamon spice

- ¼ Tbs nutmeg powder

- 2 Tbs honey

- 1 ½ Tbs cashew butter

- 8-10 ice cubes

Preparation

1. Combine skimmed milk, vanilla yogurt, cinnamon spice, nutmeg powder, honey, cashew butter, and ice cubes in the Ninja blender and mix well.

2. Pour the smoothie into tall chilled glasses and serve.

Pineapple Smoothie

Ingredients

- 2 cups canned pineapple, with juice
- 1 cup soy milk, vanilla flavor
- 1 Tbs flax seeds
- 5-6 ice cubes

Preparation

1. In the Ninja blender, add canned pineapples with juice, soy milk, flax seeds, and ice cubes and churn well.

2. Pour the smoothie into tall chilled glasses and serve.

Avocado and Raspberry Smoothie

Ingredients

- 1 Avocado, peeled and pitted
- ½ cup raspberry juice
- ½ cup orange juice
- ½ cup fresh raspberries
- 1 cup Greek yogurt, optional
- 5-6 ice cubes

Preparation

1. In the Ninja blender, add avocado, raspberry juice, orange juice, fresh raspberries, and Greek yogurt.

2. Pour the mix into tall chilled glasses and serve.

Fruity Smoothie

Ingredients

- 1 cup Greek yogurt

- 1 large banana

- 1 cup peach slices

- 1 cup pineapples, canned without juice

- ½ cup blueberries

- 1 kiwi, peeled

- 5-6 ice cubes

- ¼ Tbs cinnamon spice, optional

- mint leaves for garnish

Preparation

1. Combine Greek yogurt, banana, peach slices, pineapples, blueberries, kiwi, ice cubes in the Ninja blender and churn well.

2. Pour the smoothie into tall chilled glasses and top with a dash of cinnamon spice and garnish with mint leaves.

Spinach and Raspberry Smoothie

Ingredients

- 1 cup spinach leaves

- 1 cup frozen raspberries

- ½ orange juice

- 1 banana

- 1 cup low fat strawberry yogurt

- 6-8 baby carrots

- ¼ cup dry oatmeal

- 1-2 Tbs flax seed oil

- 8-10 ice cubes

- mint leaves for garnish

Preparation

1. In the Ninja blender, add spinach leaves, raspberries, orange juice, banana, yogurt, baby carrots, dry oatmeal, flax seed oil, ice cubes and blend well until smooth.

2. Pour the mix into tall chilled glasses, garnish with mint leaves, and serve.

Conclusion

The recipes in this book are ideal if you're considering trying to lose weight. The ingredients used in the book are low fat, high on protein and fibre content and loaded with antioxidant properties for you to feel healthy and detox.

If you choose to include Ninja blenders into your kitchen, you will be thankful to the makers, as it is unlike any other device that emits an annoying noise. Ninja blenders are not a nuisance to your ears, these blenders are designed give out a beep signal after around two minutes to let you know that the blending is done, so you need not keep checking it just to be sure.

With the simple and affordable recipes in this book, you will lose weight quickly and burn fat with these delicious and healthy Ninja Blender recipes. Of course exercise needs to be a part of your lifestyle to!

You can make any of these blended delights tonight and continue to do so for two weeks and notice a significant difference in your overall health and weight. These recipes are easy to digest and suitable for everyone.

Finally, if you enjoyed this book, then I'd like to ask you for a favor, would you be kind enough to leave a review for this book on Amazon? It'd be greatly appreciated!

Thank you and good luck!

Check Out My Other Books

Below you'll find some of my other popular books that are popular on Amazon and Kindle as well. You can visit my author page on Amazon to see other work done by me. (Josie Mackville).

Paleo Slow Cooker Cookbook

Cast Iron Cookbook

20/20 Diet Recipes

Make Ahead Meals

A Hot Sauce Cookbook

Low Temperature Recipes

Meals In A Jar Cookbook

Atkins Diet Recipes

You can simply search for these titles on the Amazon website, with my name to find them.

Want more books?

Would you love books delivered straight to your inbox every week?

Free?

How about non-fiction books on all kinds of subjects?

We send out e-books to our loyal subscribers every week to download and enjoy!

All you have to do is join! It's so easy!

Just visit the link below to sign up and then wait for your books to arrive!

www.LibraryBugs.com

Enjoy :)

Made in the USA
Monee, IL
12 October 2020